SO-ANE-367

DISCARDED

NASHVILLE PUBLIC LIBRARY

Verbs in Action
Make a Face

Dana Meachen Rau

Marshall Cavendish
Benchmark
New York

What can you make with
a paper plate, pom-poms,
crayons, and glue? You can
make anything you want.
People like gifts that you have
made.

You might follow *directions* to make something. A model sailboat comes with many parts. Directions tell you how to put those parts together.

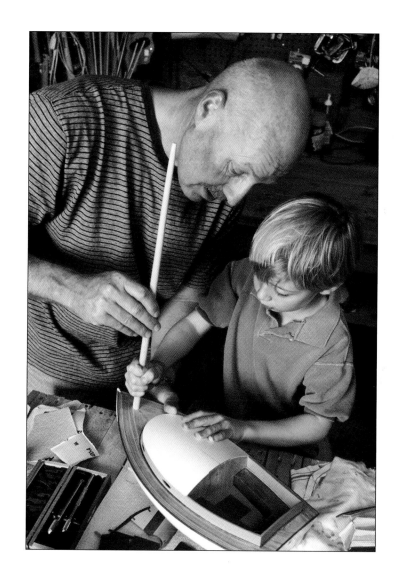

5

Recipes give directions.
A recipe tells you what
ingredients you need.

To make a cake, you need flour, sugar, butter, and eggs. You mix them together and bake it in the oven. You have made a sweet surprise!

You do not need directions
when you play make-believe.
You can make up your own
story.

You can use your *imagination*.

A house is made by many people.
Some people make the plans.
Other people make the walls
and roof.

They all work together to make it into a home.

A puzzle you play with is made by someone else. Workers make it in a *factory*. The factory sends it to a store. The store sells it to you.

Animals make things, too. Birds make nests out of sticks, grass, and mud.

Cows make milk that people drink.

Some insects make music. A cricket rubs his two front wings together to play a song.

Some plants make flowers and fruit. Some plants are vegetables.

All plants make seeds. The
seeds make new plants.

Many things make noise. A watch makes a quiet ticking sound.

A grandfather clock makes a loud bong.

It might rain on the day you planned to go to the beach. You have to "make the best of it."

If you did not bring enough snacks for everyone, you have to "make do" with what you have.

A broken toy might make you
sad. A sunny day might make
you happy.

The smell of cookies might make you hungry. Poison ivy makes you itchy.

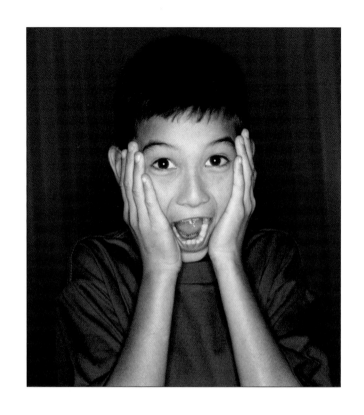

Your face tells other people how you feel. Make a happy face. Make a surprised face.

Make a scary or a silly one.

When you make something, you *express* yourself.

Do you like to make pictures? Do you like to make the winning goal? Do you like to make friends? What you make tells people a lot about you.

Challenge Words

directions (duhr-EK-shuhns)—The steps that describe how to make or do something.

express (eks-PRES)—To let others know what you think.

factory (FAK-tuhr-ee)—A place where a product is made.

imagination (i-maj-i-NAY-shuhn)—The ability to create new ideas.

ingredients (in-GREE-dee-uhnts)—The different items needed to make a certain food.

Index

Page numbers in **boldface** are illustrations.

With thanks to Nanci Vargus, Ed.D.
and Beth Walker Gambro, reading consultants

Marshall Cavendish Benchmark
Marshall Cavendish
99 White Plains Road
Tarrytown, New York 10591-9001
www.marshallcavendish.us

Text copyright © 2007 by Marshall Cavendish Corporation

All rights reserved. No part of this book may be reproduced or utilized in any form or by any means electronic or mechanical, including photocopying, recording, or by any information storage and retrieval system, without written permission from the copyright holders.

Library of Congress Cataloging-in-Publication Data

Rau, Dana Meachen, 1971-
Make a face / by Dana Meachen Rau.
p. cm. — (Bookworms. Verbs in action)
Summary: "Discusses the action described by a verb, while making connections between people and other living and nonliving objects. It also talks about other uses of the word in commonly used phrases."
—Provided by publisher.
Includes index.
ISBN-13: 978-0-7614-2290-7
ISBN-10: 0-7614-2290-0
1. Make (The English word)—Juvenile literature. 2. English language—Verb—Juvenile literature. I. Title. II. Series.
PE1317.M35R38 2006
428.1—dc22
2005026786

Photo Research by Anne Burns Images

Cover Photo by Corbis/Michael Keller

The images in this book are used with permission and through the courtesy of:
Corbis: pp. 1, 26, 27 Rob Lewine/zefa; pp. 2, 8 Jose Luis Pelaez, Inc; p. 5 Ronnie Kaufman; pp. 6, 9 Dex Images; p. 7 Royalty Free; p. 10 Corbis; p. 11 Dietrich Rose/zefa; p. 14 Roy Morsch; p. 18 Layne Kennedy; p. 19 Michelle Garrett; p. 20 H.Winkler/A.B./zefa; p. 21 Peter Harholdt; p. 22 Blasius Erlinger; p. 23 Ariel Skelley; p. 24 K.Solveig/zefa; p. 28 LWA-Dann Tardif. *SuperStock*: p. 12 Rubberball; p. 25 age footstock. *Photo Researchers, Inc.*: p. 17 Gilbert S. Grant.

Printed in Malaysia
1 3 5 6 4 2